A WINTER'S TAIL
Book Three of The Weasel Chronicles

by KS Green

To order additional copies of this book, contact:
Xlibris
844-714-8691
www.Xlibris.com
Orders@Xlibris.com

ISBN: Softcover   978-1-5992-6758-6
        Hardcover   978-1-4797-1867-2
        EBook   978-1-6641-9383-3

Library of Congress Control Number: 2005908444

Print information available on the last page

Rev. date: 09/02/2021

★ Well Well ★

Well ... well ... so that's it then ? ... one mr Weasel ... one flurried snowful frigid storm ... a nippy brisk camofreeze out ... and another unexplained cool melting away of this one mr Weasel into the positively pale blundering unqualified icy white prevailing overwhelmic background ... what utter unmitigated double distilled all fired up pure proper straight out uninhabited vacuous vacancy was this all about ?!?! ... anyway ? ...

i for one have had it ... over and up to my nose with this ... what does this Weasel think we are all doing ? ... walking around on idiomatic ? ... as if we can't even think or something ...

* thanks allie u. for the weasel's framed art

★ Blankety Blank ★

Okay ... i'll show this Weasel what thinking is all about ... all i have to do is read the evening Daily Blank ... they always tell me what to think ... it is all right there in the opinion column ... i just opiate the paper to the right page ... and ... and ... filiblustering filigreed flounders ! ... why do these blankety Blank pages always stick together ? ... cheesewilbercurds ! ... i'm tired of always getting ripped off ... take that ... and this ... and this and

that ... and ... oops ... there went the Blank ... dang ! ...

now i'll have to read another book ... hmmm ... what's this ? ... A Winter's Tail ... curious very courteous ...

★ Time Fur That ★

Well ... i guess another book isn't really so bad ... besides i have had a busy day and i need to sit and relax a bit ... at least i'm not the one who has to write it ... so let's see what's going on now ... oh ... this one is about that dern Weasel too ... a useless creature that one ...

page one ... and so it had come to pass ... spring had become summer ... summer ... autumn ... and autumn had passed into winter ... and with it came the snow ... and the chillies ... and the timeless ritual of the weasels ... the changing of the coat ... it was time fur that all again ...

★ White Out ★

Yes ... it were times like all that once again ... winter had arrived ... and me ... our mr Weasel extraordinaire ... had changed my chic beige fur white ... as if in my present predicament it made any defense what colour i stood in fur ... for i was now totally engulped by a slavouring white cloud out snow fall that had arrived to storm around me out of contol ... i must check my position for inside these swirls i could easily disappear ... and as far as i could remember ... i was hoping not to do that again ...

i consulted my Globular Audio Symbolic Partitioning System ... the GASPS what a great invention ... swizzles in any and all barometric conditions with vary little unsympathetic sycophancy due to magnetic distractions ... got mine at a discount sale at the UNWWMM slurplus store in downtown Weaslton ... i felt a warm rush of renewable confidence as i nosed my face into the wind ...

★ Here Now ★

Let's see ... i knew my last position to within twenty million solar systems ... for we keep records you know ... but one sweep of my Globular Audio Symbolic Partitioning System would narrow that down quickly enough ... here ... here ... here ... it sqwelched ... by the sound of it ... i could have mistaken my invisible surrounding for the Athenian Senate ... time ... maybe 800 BC ... was i making a speech or something ? ... but i knew better ... my GASPS was announcing i was here ... and the time ... i checked ... now ... here and now ... hmm ... must be the sixties ... had i stumbled into a time warp on accident ? ... but the insistence of my device read out other wise ... i really was here now ...

i checked my journal ... i had crossed the Rug Savannah under the intense glare of the summer sun ... west by west west ... skittered and battled across the Linoleum Flats ... east by east east ... hither... thither ... Mary ... Junior ... Violet ... X ... Denile ... many entries ... many options ... many variables ... i entered them all and waited for the answer to dis-solve ... so all in all ... that comes out to ...West East by ignor' West of South North Weast by Snorth Wouth ...

★ unFinnisht Steppes ★

Which put me just at the base of the unFinnisht Steppes ... munchen Mongols ! ... i muttered as the wind tore the mumbles from my words ... do the heavens give not a break uponst wee wandering weasels ? ... a heart wrenching question i would have to answer sometime ladder ... half the galaxy i had already roamed when i once ambled unawares onto the Snooze Plateau ... and now this ... hurdle ... which i had to climb because it was here ... between me and there

... and in the midst of winter ... too ...

i checked my mountaineering gear ... perhaps i should wear something a little more upbeat ... some colourful garb to counter offset my bleary surroundings ... perhaps something with a tinkling Tibetan flavour ... for i was headed for the high country ... after all ... and one should dress appropriately ... au cause de you could never know whom one might meet ... or for what occasion one whom should be preprepped for ...

★ Up The Steppes ★

But it was superfluouse to preprepp too far into the foreseeable ahead, i knew ... for the great challenge of the unFinnisht Steppes loomed above me beforehand and feet ... and what a loom it was ... i would rather have knitted spinning tales of the perils of the Rug than to launch myself upon it ... but the time had come to up the Steppes onto the next level ... so bravely i ventured aforth ...

i could have waited and gone
with a fifth ... a few snorts of my favorite fermented fruit juice would have eased the passage quite nicely ... but i was feeling weasely and impatient ... and waiting was not on my agenda ...

★ CatChungba Icefall ★

What was on my agenda was ... getting up the CatChungba icefall in one piece ... already i had more than likely gone an icebrige too far ... a wrong steppe in any fragile direction could lead to an immediate breakdown ... and there would be an all out but good chance of getting nooked or crannied into a crevasse ... or torrented away into a wild untamed schluggling river of boulders and snow melt to be spilled helpless upon the tributary flood plains of the holy Brahmapooter ... or at minimum i might tumble off the steppes and into a stupid old toolbox ...

but i had long mastered sure footedness some years ago ... before i left the monastery ... then i had tip-pawed across an entire floor covered with rice paper ... and waltzed away with a free fish dinner ... without getting snarled ... i had learned much ... certainly ... i removed my tinkling bells ... for a single sound could set the ice to cackling ... and what a disaster an out break of giggles might ensure ... i broke out of the clouds at an altitude of just over 19 thousand millimeters ... into a cold clear calm wind ... the sun flipped out precious little heat at this altitude ... i stood transfixed by what i was seeing but should not ... the vestiges of a previous ascending experdition ... a fixed rope ...

★ Fixed Rope Strings Attached ★

And don't think i wasn't thankful ... not much good would a broken rope do to me ... but there camest along with it all a feeling of uneasy business ... had some weasel been here before ? ... fixed the rope ... and then casually left it hanging about ? ... as if leaving an inviting temptation ... would there be strings attached ? ... the likelyhood was high ...

should i partake of the windfall rope ? ... but i was a pragmanical purist ... my normal mode of praxis was free form alpinism ... so how could i ? ... a brief moment of perplextifiliation followed ... but i broomed back sweepingly and efficiently with a plan ... i would coil the rope up as i climbed along next-side to it ... thus by solving the enigmasticky issue on the spot ... and getting some free rope at the same time ... i was clever after all was said and begun ...

★ End Of My Rope ★

But no sooner had i begun when i realized that all was still amiss ... the rope hadn't been fixed after all ... for it would not come away from the wall ... perhaps it was attached ... ropes were for coiling and wrapping up ... and things ... and it wasn't doing those things ... my conclusion wisely was it must still be broken ... which meant i better not use it ... what if it were to break ? ...

oh well ... i decided to follow it instead ... i knew better than to pull threads ... snore boarding could not be accomplished on such perilous ground as where upon i stood ... it was imperative that i must clambrr higher ... perhaps there would be an answer at the other end ... or perhaps not ... i hadn't a clue ... but after some effort and a damp brow ... when i reached the end of my rope ... that's all that was there ... that and the confounded endless steppes ...

Endless steppes ... and ... a winding road that leopard across into the distance ... the snow had thinned allowing an invisible air that lingered away towards a far line of mountains ... perhaps the steppes were not endless after all ... for after all i had climbed to the nippy tippy top of the CatChunba icefall ... and was now in the homelands of the ... the ... mon gnashy nosh ! ... now i knew why i felt the uneasy business ! ... what kind of an plundered witted feather nosed nincomweaselpoop ninny brain was i ? ...

and i had been so easily roped up into it ... fiddle snouts ! ... wouldn't you know it ... right smack dabbled in the diddle of it all ... the home of the lurky Himal snow cat Leo padres ! ... i put on a defensive bell and tipped my monastical staff with its brass ...

★ Um How Mani Padres Humm ? ★

Born under the sign of the great slumbering lion of the winter constellations ... the fierce spotty snow cat Leo padres had in early eons migrated up the steppes ... and now freely reigned mainly on the plain ... but as fortune would have it ... i had recently read up on them ... and was imbibed with the full fruits of my knowledge ... i would delicately de-inebriate my learning with grace ... for she had taught me

well ... the Leo padres could be fierce ... unless ... one approaches them correctly ...

and here were two now ... ambling the road of wisdom ... dressed to the hilt as was the habit of their strange denominator ... chanting their exotic questioning purana chant ... Um How Mani Padres Humm ? ... Purrrrr ... i was uneasy ...

★ **Two Too Mani** ★

I thought like i did with grace ... but not about her like i usually did ... the answering chant was easy ... and i softly reverberated with it ... Two Too Mani Padres Humm ... oops ... i must have said it wrong for the gentle irritated roar of eternity interrupted into the great indestructible stillness ... oh ummmmm ... maybe it was just ...Two Mani Padres Humm ? ... the roar continued ...

it seemed to come from far away beyond all matter and anti-matter ... like the esscenls of existence ... or from deep within some earthen bowls ... as if exposing the worldly phenomena of all change and unbecoming ... it was folding and unfolding and very revealing out of the steppes in a timeless drama of mystery and wonder ... but even so ... perhaps i was right ... maybe there were two too many spotty Himal snow cat Leo padres ... for comfort ... it now seemed like a good time for a lecture about keeping onto the road to peaceful enlightenment ... but i could see these two carikittitures had already strayed from the path of good will ... i slipped into my Tibetan tourist outfit and belled my point ...

★ Do You Speak Weasel ? ★

Which was a smart move considering they were presently misunderstanding right in the middle of my way ... i had long ago learned the art of being a stranger ... for i held many years of experience being stranger in stranger lands than this ... always appear non-hostile ... and above all ... never admit to knowledge of the local tongue ... for your hosts will not speak freely to each other in their own dialect if they suspect you can understand their insults ... or know why they are laughing at you ... nor will they give you proper directions if you have lost your way ... the snow had re-begun again to silently whisker from the clouds above ... i joined in with the roar of eternity with the suitable chant ... but only as an introduction ...

oh ummmmm ... i kept my palms up so they would know i was just an empty handed weasel and was not posed to be dangerous ... oh ummmmm ... excuse me ? ... do you speak weasel ? ... i am a tourist ... i showed them my camera ... a tourist on the way ... i emphasized the so there could be no possible doubt as to which the way i was going ... but i seem to have lost it... i seek oneness ... and perhaps a good nap ? ... then maybe re-enlightening in the morning ... and a cup of your world famous tea ? ... i am not ordinary common you see ... i have friends ... i know the High Brr himself ... oh ummmm ... maybe i should have mentioned the High Brr right off the bat instead of all this chanting around the dishes ... for no sooner had i mentioned His Wholly Coolness than the Himal snow cat Leo padres zippered away like an enthreatened species ... nary a spot of them remained ... just the usual couple of disappear-o-puffs ...

★ Zen We Can Go Now ? ★

I looked around the great expanse of empty nothingness that surrounded my selfless awareness ... and as the snow whiffled down to soft wickets on the ground ... i took a couple of super snaps ... which could have been better ... if only the snow Leo padres had stuck about and acted naturally as if the camera weren't there ... then i would at least have had some interesting depth of field ... oh well ...

i broke the gap and spoke into the silence ... sending a few simple hopeful words into the great avoidance ... oh ummmmm ... zen we can go now ?...

★ The Straight And Narrow ★

Apparently it was okay to leave ... but the road ... the one true straight and narrow highway ... it is so long its been good to know you ... and very twisty and winding and difficult and bumpy ... not at all like on the maps they give you with the pretty little pictures ... how could i travel such a difficult passage solely afoot ? ... i consulted my travel guide ... one of the perks of being disguised as a tourist ...

the answer was obvious ... after all ... i had acquired noodles of mileage award discounts and plenty of coupons ... why not use them ?... i would just have to rent transport and drive up the road of all knowingness ... or wait for the bus ... which ever i could figure out first ... i packed up my point and added a few more bells for good measure ... and prepared for a wait ...

★ Good Karmabile ★

Which turned out not to be very long ... and required very little figuring on my part ... because i knew the answer would rapidly arrive self evidentually ... which it promptly did ... which was quite fortunate because i had just missed my train of thought ... and my schedule showed none other due for some time ... i snapped out of worrying about it though ... as an exquizzically decorated karmabile slid to a stop with a sqwoosh of tires ... the snow was nearly flundering down by now ...

and luck really was with me ... there was this great weaselette at the wheel ... for it was a good karmabile ... i had heard terrifying stories in the dives of Catmangodoo about the bad ones ... i never wanted the experience of riding in one of them personified in my memoirs ... not only that ... but the sign announced that it was going to Snorway even ... i tossed my gear atop and folded my flag stick which broke into two ...

★ On The Snorway Highway ★

Some things are just too good to be true ... so i played with the thought that maybe this wasn't really happening ... i tossed that one out right quickly ... it was so bad it could be true ... but no ... this was a true good ... and i wanted to keep it that way ... no negative thoughts for the great vacumn cleaner of existence to inhale and then exhale back on me ... what to say though ? ... do you often drive here ? ... what's a hot weaselette like you driving high on the way like this ? ... no ... not very original ... i would have to do better ...

do you snow the way to sand Snorway ? ... geezwishkers ... how dumb ... she's the blipping driver ... if she doesn't know the way we're all in big trouble ... i decided to play it safe and open with the old standard by-the-way ... oh ummmmm ... nice weather we're having ... eh ? ...

★ She Sqweaked ★

It's a flundering fizzling blizzard ! ... you flipping weasel ! ... she sqweaked in a smooth liquid mellow sort of way ... wha ? ... wha ? ... i stammered ... you ... you ... you sqweaked !... of course i sqweaked ! ... she sqweaked ... you one-sixteenth of a brained weasel ... the rest was lost in muttering ... i thought of Vana ... she never sqweaked ...

but ... but ... weaselettes just look cute and stuff ... i ventured boldly ... they can't sqweak ! ... it would mean they had to think first ... and everyone knows ... but i was cut off in mid-proclamation by all kinds of sputtering sounds ... i looked behind my seat ... did one of those snow cat Leo padres sneak in here when the door was open ? ... no ... oh ummmmm ... it must have been the wind ...

But no ... it wasn't the wind either ... my new friend seemed to be holding her breath because her face was rapidly turning the colour of her hair ... these yoga weaselettes ... i thought with admiration ... what self control they had ... now when it came to me ... what self control ? ... that was the norm ... oh well anyway ... there were much more important things to worry about than breathing exercises ... for i could see we were now driving through the very extreme famous Snorweigan Woods ... oh Weasel ! ... how exciting ... too bad about the Beatle infestation problem ...

do you think we can stop for a picture at Sleepy Hollow ? ... i asked ... and maybe an iced spruce cone ? ... but she was still deep in the purple trance and didn't seem able of a coherent response at this juncture in the road ... no big macadamian wheeled deal ... i didn't really need another trunkful of photographic memories cluttering up my brain ... just to have been here is thrill enough ...

PAWS 1

★ Worry About Outback ★

'ello mateys ... good on ya cobbled ... nice to see ya rootin' ... we'll just toss ol' barbie on the grill an' pop a few brews ... that's they way we like to do it down under wear the roos kan ga where they like ... s'fur certain ... make's ya feel at hum like ... well ... i kin see ya'r been troopin' a wee too long abouts in the Himals ... eh ? ... gets about ta feeling all dingoed out ... so why spend all yer time walkarounding up in them highlands beset with frets ?... when yah kin pack up all yer cares and woes ... swing em low... and bring em on down across to the great country and contentment of Weastrailia ?... woylie brushtailed bettongs we'll have a good ol' time ...

picture you in this ... a brand new pair of all terrain rubber boot weaselbies ... gatorsnake skin tuxedo with matching marsupial trowsers and wombat trim ... corker bowler ta keep the flies from flyin' up yew nose where ... bag o' complimentry malt whiskey weasel beer puffs ... your own abosoluteliorginal guide ... just you ... and all your vexitating problems ... yew'll drive the shielas wild ... the bilbies'll be hopping all over you ... now ya'r ready ta dijerydo down ... let's go worry about outback ... sure as snuff we'll all sing matilda ... it'll be super grand ... just think of the agitation and anxiety yu'll experience while trampling under the endless stars what glitter outback in ol' Ganwanderland ... a place for true world class worrying ... book now while your bookie is cookin' ... Weastrailian Abosolutelioriginal Trampling Worry About Outback Sahfaris ... or call us toll free at WatWaoS and we'll reverse the charges ... good on about ya ...

★ High Brr Highlands ★

But now the road began to climb ... outside of the windscreen i could see the terraces of the High Brr Highlands coolly marching up to make their appointment with the High Brr Cliffs as the Snorway highway hair pinned its dicey coiffure up to the permed tundra of the High Brr Nation itself ... there were few vehicles on the road ... and all the drivers seemed to stick to a very rudimentary code of trying to shove you over the edge ... the snow was thinning as we gained altitude ...

i kept my nose wide awake ... i spotted a rare blue horned pink mountain goat ... and made a note in my journal ... but it was too far away for a good photo ... and my telephoto was packed in my pack which was packed upstairs on top with my rope ... well ... never matter, i reminded myself ... i'm not working for the International Weasyographic ...with luck we would be browsing through the gabled gates of lost Tidbit's fabled table top plain before nightfall ... i hoped we would fare there well ... for i had not had a bite for well over an hour ... and Tidbit was famous for its nibbles ...

★ Weasel's Arrival ★

We crested with a wave of my monastery flags over onto the high Tidbit topside ... it was a moment that would be difficult to topple in future years ... the sky wasn't dark or heavy ... nor was it grey ... there was no snow falling ... the wind wasn't a deep nasty stinging bitter icy cold ... there weren't swirls of frost dancing mysteriously and threatening-like across the road ... the grass wasn't ponderous with ice globulars ... and the well manicured irrigation channels were not lumbering under a cumbersome shrouded frozen crust ... the numberous peasants toiling contentedly through massive snow drifts under the weight of each individual's predetermined fate-for-this-lifetime were not numberous ... in fact there were none about at all ... nor were the snow drifts massive or about either ...

all that was about were the curious eyes of a great stupa temple that stooped partially out of stupid sight across a canal ... what's up ? i thought ... such an acclaimed event as Weasel's Arrival should not go unnoticed ... something must be going on ...

★ Honey Bee Knot Hostel ★

I was dumped unceremoniously at the door step of my darling little back nappers hostel ... the Honey Bee Knot Hostel ... and my good karmabile driver spurned off down the empty rue with a spindle of tires flinging dust grovels ... oh ummm ... i wonder what that was all about ? ... i was pensive ... but other motivators were busy getting me inside the door ... i picked pack and rope up ... and marched into the lobby ...

18

like the missing peasants there was no one in here also ... hellooo it is i ... i called as if answering my home nest telephone ... it is a sure way to get respectful attention ... to behave not only as if you belonged where you are ... but also act as if you knew why you are there too ... page so and so of the basic tourist survival guide ... hellooo ... but there was no answer ...

★ Check in Knot ★

How odd ... i thought wryly as i approached the check-in desk warily ... i dinged upon the bell and waited ... re-dinged and re-waited ... well isn't this just special ... i laid my hands upon the counter with Weasel authority and brushed onto a newspaper ... i picked it up ... the Daily Lamah ... i placed the headlines in front of my nose ...

Big Speech Today ... interesting ... i read further on and arrived at a picture ... the High Brr himself ... i glanced at the caption ... it was the winter State of the High Brr Nation speech ... apparently it was a national holiday and everyone woke up for it ...

★ Geezkrishnanewts ★

Geezkrishnanewts ... i'm awake ... i thought ... well i better get down there, too ... otherwise they may think i had been brought up with ill mannerisms ... i left my gear behind the counter with a note explaining who i was ... with explicit and detailed instructions not to steal my stuff ... and nippered off ...

i high weaseled it through the narrow streets down to the town square where everything was getting up to it ... and arrived just nicking the moment in the spur of time ... for the great big speech was already starting to be addressed ... as we speak ...

★ State Address ★

My fellow High Brr natives ... let it be knownst far and width much definitiveness ... that our greatly landed High Brr Nation is not one what is afraid to dream ...far from it ... we are not teeth gnashers in the face of the new horizon ... wow ... i thought ... great words ... uplifting ... full of hops ... i listened closer since i was way in the back ... and could hardly see ...accidentally bumping my noggin on the wall ... we live in a time of cavalcading culinary breakthroughs ...through which some of us may find it difficult to snooze ... fresh baked croissants wafting upon the airwaves of Tidbit brings much disturbances to our sensitive slumber patterns ... rest assured with your doubts ... while you sleep your governmentals monitor the situation religiously in the kitchens of power ... i know there is much munch compensation we mustard offer all ... for these fragrances vista upon us all ... so we shall mandate all our accessories upon the embellished axiom of these trying thymes ... so shallot be ...

what sangfroid his wholly coolness reprimands of his subjects ... not only does he research them all ... but they listen too ... my eyes glistened with pride at being a weasel ... which was way off the point and had nothing to do with anything at the moment ... but that didn't matter ... it was a flag waving moment ... so let us join together in the oneness of all that is one ... and think not what Tidbits can do good for you ... nay i say ... dare to dream ... think what good nibbles you can do with Tidbits in our glorious High Brr Nation ... roses and reincarnations to us all ... oh and by the way has anyone noticed where the snow went ? ...

★ Bustle For Lunch ★

Just like the great High Brr to leave us with such a magnolian magnanimous question to ponder on and to cajole ... what magnificence ... while the rest of the world hustles about their lowly doings of this and that and those ... he leaves radiating us with these incandescent thoughts ... such eternal contemplations ...

oh ummm ... i wonder where the snow did go ? ... i wondered ... could we ever really know ? ... did we as humble weasels have that capacity ? ...but there was no whom to ponder on this with ... for now all the colourful Low Brrs had gone hastily back to their own business ... leaving the once tumultuous square a circle of emptiness ... perhaps it was lunch time ? ... i had an unexpected instant revelation ... somewhere it is always lunchtime ... now that was a cheery thought ... maybe it was happening right now at the Honey Bee Knot ... i decided to bustle back that way before it was over ... but upon my brow ! ... it was starting to snow ...

★ I Snew It ★

I had much to wonder about on my way to the hostel ... oh ... i get it ...i said when i finally got it ... it was a rhetorical question that one about the snow ... its here ... its always here ... basically ... like clouds ... like water ... the eternal cycle of vapour to water to water vapour ... how clever ... and by the time i trompled into the lobby i snew the answer ... i really did ... it was so clear ... and cloudy ... at the same time ... that was it ... and now it really

was ... a blizzard again ... but i snew that all along ... too ...

i swirled on up to the counter ready to have a word with the whom whom was in charge ... but there was a debate happening between several whoms about my note and my unmistakably exact directions to the reader ... apparently they agreed i was Weasel ... but there was considerable disagreement and laughter on whether i was serious about not stealing all my possessions ... Harrumph, may i say ! ..and did loudly ... a mute point ... now that i was here in person right under the noses ...

★ A Summons ★

Well ... that muted all that nonsense ... and that simplified matters a whole lot ... the whoms settled down ... and you are mr Weasel we presume ? ... said they ... aye said i ... there is a message for you ... i was handed a piece of paper ... a notice ? ... had i been fired ? ... but who could replace me ? ... i was Weasel ! ... this was outrageous ... i would write my representative in the House of Weasels ... organize a march ... proclaim a day ... Weasel Day ...

by weasel ! ... i opened the note ... oh ...

it wasn't a notice i noticed after all ... it was a summons ... the High Brr heard i was in town and was requesting my attendance at the palace ... rsvp not required ... for you will be there ... oh ... well in that case ... i guess i better will be there tonight ... i checked the time ... geologically speaking it was probably half past the Pleistocene Age ... if i made haste i could get there before nightfall ... or at least prior to the next massive expansion of glaciers ...

★ Best Of Rooms ★

I signaled one of the whoms ... be a good whom chap and deposit my baggage ... i used the Francois pronunciation naturally ... in my chambre ... if you would be so kind ... i must jump into le douche to freshen up before my ... ahem ... dinner appointment with ... oh ummm ... the High Brrness ... that got a reaction such as has not been seen of since the snow cat Leo padres made a quick exit some pages ago ... i was swiffled off to the best of rooms within eye blinks ... with a grand overlook out the window ...

i gave them a special grateful tip about how to mix a great curry con largo ... but they refused to accept it ... when i insisted ... they wouldn't hear about it ... where in the weasel world can you get service like that anymore ? ... at least in this age today ? ... everybody wants something for nothing usually ... i surveyed my room after the whoms were left ... there was the window and a rather dismal poster of a blizzard which was a bit too art newveau for me ... what do Brrs see in it ? ... i wondered

... and a shower right next to the open window ... whom would want to pin a window so close to la douche ? ... i figured it was a cultural thing ... at least there is blue and pink running water ... dang ... i was really hoping for some good'n red running water ... i sighed ...

PAWS 2

★ Weasel Night School ★

Is life getting you down ? ... well maybe it is time to get down ! ... so come on down to the University of Weaslonia night school and re-enrole for some exciting new courses ... where you have the choice ! ... why weasel away your precious hours doing constructive things ? ... when you can be spending your weasel dollars and time to obtain this once in a lifetime Weasel Certificate ? ... with this certificate you'll be able to go out into the world and start weaseling all over again ... from square zero ... but this time with a

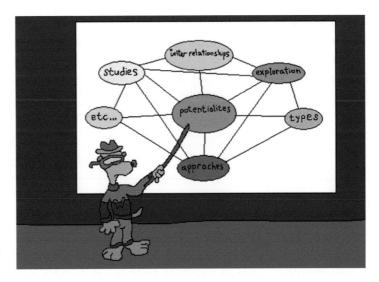

piece of paper stamped with the Weasel Dot of Determination ... it will provide you with a comprehensive exploration of the interrelationships between types ... it will highlight potentialities ... etc ... and demonstrate uniquely integrated approaches positively ... whom can ask for more ? ...

learn how everything ties together in real slide projections ... ellipse graphs with bar-line connectors make everything fit and understandable ... but its not all work ... when you're not nosing down an intensive dessertation ... why not pop into our on-campus gymnasium and press charges for an hour ? ... you'll feel great afterwards ... full time Weasel Degree programmes start every two minutes until the end of the hour ... so hurry and enroll now ! ... major and some minor credible cards are often accepted ... but you must enquire or further details will be withheld ...

★ What To Wear ★

One thing about pink water is that you're in and out of le shower a lot quicker ... brrr ... i probably would have been quicker anyway with an open window right there ... don't whoms have any modesty ? ... but cultural differences is what really makes our lives interesting ... just think if we all used the same big mcWeasel soap bar the world around ... how boring ... there would be no need to go shower anywhere but where ever you shower ...

but there was need now ... the sun was slipping ... and the next ice age was only ten thousand years away ... and i would musts be at the palace by night tumble ... but what to wear ? ... difficult ... very difficult ... something a bit snappy with a brush stroke of a frosted nip around the edges ? ... a classichill style perhaps somewhat dated as if frozen in time ? ... brisk colours with a crisp cut ... bracing but not frigid ... altogether cool ... but formal enough to fit the occasion ...

★ Weaselly's Jeepers ★

I think a nice carrot sort of rounds it out ... i thought while balancing one on my nose ... but that didn't actually work seeing how i kept eating them ... okay okay ... forget it ... i wobbled down the stairs and sort uv rolled to a halt at the desk ... my good whom ... yes ... you there ... i am in need of transport to the palace ... i rapped my walking flag stick on the counter for effection ... you can never know with these lower Brr types i reminded myself prudely ...

a taxicabal pulled secretively over up out by the door ... wow ... a Weaselly's Jeepers ... i hadn't seen one of them since Norman's Day ... a bit airy for the circumstances i thought ... but weather or not isn't everything ... the whoms slushed me aboard in a sleeting ... thanks ... i said ... and was starting to give them a comraderly tip about creamed spinach carrot soufflé ... but once again they wouldn't hear of it ... not like back in the good old UN of W ... i gave the gal the address ... le palace ... s'livervousplease ... oh jeepers ... its you ! ...

★ Shivered Off To The Palace ★

And it was her you ... how ddo ? ... she was wearing an outrageous hat ... from where i was sitting as i looked around myself ... perhaps i should pre-tip her something about modern fashion ... but i decided not to ... i didn't want her to get her avant guard up right away ... i decided to be a bit more tactful ... after all ... she was looking a little better than the last time we met ... not off colour like she had been afore ... ice supposed i should come up with something a little more savoir ... the weather worked last time ... tried true and blue chip ... oh ummm ... nice blizzards you have here in Tidbit ... i hazarded ... eh?

she spluggered a smupffled sqweak ... geeziteverywhere ... i didn't even know spluggered was a word ... but her colour seemed to remain in the stable ... traffic was light to none as we jerked from the curble ... she was a she driver so i remained very understanding ... not not paticularily partially panicked ... but understanding none or less ... and so we shivered off to the palace ...

★ Curbed Again ★

After many near misses and practical head-on collisions with the missing traffic ... during which i was constantly saying things like yikes and ohmigush ... and the Honey Bee said naught but grumbles ... we safely sqweegeed on a stopper outside the palace steppes ... i may have melted a little in the heat of the moments ... in as much as i noticed my curbed spill out was easier than the spill in ... i seemed a tad thinner ...

i boobbled on the pavement again and was just reaching for a good tip about a yam quiche flambé ... when she did it again ... spurned off with a splindle of tires ... this time flinging snow grovels ... i'll have to have a serious parlez-vous with this whomette next time ... definitely ... i gazed up the palace steppes ... luckily there were only a few ... and with great will ... i willed my self to snowball forward ...

★ The Red Carpet ★

Well ... getting up the staircase was not a pretty sight for sore thighs ... but i made it with moderate gracefulness ... i lost a few more degrees around the waist from all the aerobics ... and was actually feeling evaporated by the time i reached the Grand guarded entrance Hall ... can't say i liked the looks of those two scruffies ... i thought ... then announced myself in true weasel fashion ...

ahem ... royal hands ... it is i ... Weasel ... extraordinaire ... graduate cum loudly so they could hear ... arrived for my oddition with the Highness ... i held out my summons ... the red carpet did not escape my notice ... fitting indeed ... a little damp though ... and i wondered what a rug was doing with three coal buttons ... didn't make much sense to me ... but there was an inviting warm coloured glow at the end of the hall ... which did ...

★ Floored Em ★

I ushered myself towards it ... while composing a little as i crossed the threshold ... i'm a winky dinky Weasel winky dinky do or die dum dumb ... well that was enough for now ... i stepped into the lemon coloured warm lime light ... and with a floor-ish slipped elegantly nose first onto the freshly polished tiles ... my ushering momentum carried me in a graceful slide across the Great Grand Hall and deposited myself in a fine mosaic at the foot of the throne ... floored 'em again ... i thought ...

standing up seemed inappropriate and waxed a difficult prospect ... so i retained my fine urbane sprawl ... as it was appropriate and well pre-postureous for my interview ... okay ... so maybe it was a bit of an awkward entrance ... but no one mentioned the red carpet treatment would end so quickly at the doorway ... and whom waxed the tiles so heavily ? ... but master of quick improvisation as i was ... i cornered it all to my advantage ... i am here ... oh honored High cool Brrness ... your terrificly amazing extravagantly humble diplomaticly envoyed stupendous Weasel fantastique ... although i pronned in correct manner ... one must let whom know who is what ...

★ Parley Views ★

If i waited to speak until spoken to ... i would be at this hearing long after silence had come and passed far into fossils ... i melted first with a fine gambit ... oh ummm ... Hail All ... what is it that you require here of my oddience ? ... shall we parley views ? ...

a verifiable barrage of utterances avalaunched in my direction in billowing flurries ... i sat up and turned to my interpreter ... and the High Brr said what ? ... the strange contraption stared at me momentarily ... then spewed out a raffle of parchment ...

★ Pray Tell ★

Pray tell what this is all about ? ... i thought widely ... and grasping this strange raffle in the clutches of my interest i became astonished ... for it was written in the vernacular of the ancient High Brr Nation ... a drowsy dozy dialect ... a lethargic lackluster languid language ... not heard from on tongues since ... oh ... autumn i guess ... what could this parch have meant ? ... i couldn't read a flake of it ... let alone understand it ... besides it made me feel sloomy all over ... i was nodding off ...

i'm in for it now ... i murmured confidentusually to myself who nodded in agreement ... oops ... the High Brr took this misunderstandingly for understanding ... for another snowslide of expletives fuselaged in my direction ... and the translator whirled ... and the raffles flew ... maps ... directions ... orders ... decrees ... mandates ... commandments ... dictates ... biddings ... any requests ? ...

★ What Alight Through Yawnder Blinks ★

Do you know down by the Weasely River ? ... i asked the guards as i was unceremoniously bustled out of the Great Grand haul ... it seemed my meeting was over and finis ... along exotic dimly lit passageways i was handled ... only vaguely aware of my soreroundings .... i could not see ... but i could smell ... hmm ... we passed the kitchen ... i raised my eyebrows hintfully ? for i was in the mood for some food related activity ... but the obvious was lost on these two uncouths ... whom passed the tanglizing smell of wafting fresh baked eating things as if oblivious to the edible ...

i was unhandled at the back doorknob ... the whole entire wrangle of parchment raffles was wordlessly stuffed into my paws and i was pushered outside ... the door banged precisely nearby my rear ... causing a jump ... so now what ? i wondered

landing adroitly ... but my now whatting was disturbed by the exsploittering sound of an engine's motor blurting out a start ... and blinking red and green alights ... what alight through yawnder blinks ? ...

★ The Engine's Motor ★

Well ... weasel to weasel ... there was only one way to find out ... by crossing yawnder ... i put my raffles in my very convenient very rare laconic skin brief case for ease of handling ... and zipped on my long sleeves and pants legs to combat the chill ... and set off ... it was a fine evening ... just a hint of dew ice basking on the grass as if pretending not to be frozen like everything else ... i ran with my toes through it ... and then i was sliding along on the hard glassy smooth of a lake ... how wonderful ... i reflected on this momentarily ... well ice is a lot like a mirror ... so it stands well within reasoning ...

but i came rapidly to yawnder's end quiet quickly ... when i bumped into the source of yawnder's flipping blinking alights ... and the exploittering engine's motor ... t'id belong to an airplane ...

PAWS 3

★ **UNWFBEFAFRRSBST** ★
Scenario 1

Hello my good and right true stalwart friends ... hereinst follows a brief introinduction to what you can expect if you join up with the Unified Nests of Weaslonia Fire Brigade Emergency First Aid First Respondent Rescue Standby Backup Support Team ... the UNWFBEFAFRRSBST ... you gotta be big to wear our emblem ... snap shot this ! ... a wanton fire breaks out of the old mill at the Weaselly River ferry crossing ... and you are recalled upon out from weaseling along normally to reel it in ... you are the only UNWFBEFAFRRSBST member for nearly ever around ... what do you do ? ...

scenario one : you have no training whatso ever (see images above ... events taken from actually occurred happenstances) ... mr Weaseldoe (first name john withheld for security purposes) sees the fire jumping out from the mill ... spends valuable moments alarming others nearby ... sees a handy bucket ... sees the convenient river ... scoops up water with little or no thought ... and puts out the fire ... damage is minimal ... the ferries are exstatic as only ferries can be ... not pleasant ... but as shocking as this may seem ... things like this happen unchecked and out of our control on a frighteningly daily basis just about all over the place ...

Scenario 2

But there is really no need to feel disparaged ... now ... for on the other instance ... imagine yourself in the same situation fully trained and experted in the ways of the UNWFBEFAFRRSBST ... you are weaseling along at your own natural level of normalcy ... when a fire comes bounding from the old mill where the ferries cross the Weaselly River ... this in itself is enough to raise an eyebrow ... but you snap immediately into action nothing-the-less ...

scenario two : you are full of it and on par with the latest pyromanic techniques of the UNWFBEFAFRRSBST ...
you remember about things from your intensive training automentally as if your second nature has gotten the better of you ... you realize your first duty is not to alarm anybody ... so you don't ... a calm scene is a cool site ... you do not act impulsively without prior consideration of your actions ... you run down your mental check list ... 1) you gather facts ... you noted there was a bucket ... and a convenient river ... these could be useful in an emergency ... and you file that important knowledge away ... 2) you consider priorities ... is the welfare of a bunch of ferries really that important ? ... what about the mill ? is it mostly wood or greatly of stone ? ... will taking water out of the river disturb the fish fry ? is there a fish fry ? ... if so, why wasn't i invited ? ... 3) you access your situation ... if i wasn't invited ... surely i should have been ... stands to reason ... i'm probably the only truly trained rescue weasel for all the roundabouts here ... 4) you establish priorities ... firstly the fire probably needs to be put out ... then the ferries should be tied up and seen to or analyzed or something ... or the other way around would also work ... you

make a mental tick ... 5) you make decisions ... uh ... someone really should do something ... at a minimum at least ... okay ... let's do that then ...you figger ... hey why not ? ... i'm the Weasel ... 6) you develop a plan of action ... i'll go check the bucket ... if there's a hole in the bucket ... then i'll fix it ... with a straw if the axe ain't too dull ... but if it is then i'll sharpen it with a stone ... if i can find one and its not too dry ... but if it is then i'll wet it with water from the river ... oh my dear weary elieza what a mess ... how will i get water ? ... no problem ... there might not be a hole in the bucket ... but what if there is ? ... but no time for all that now ... for now ... 7) you take action ... yes it is that time ... but you are well prepared mentally ... for you have fortified yourself with all kinds of worst case scenarios prior to them ... if any one or more or less of them turn out to be happening ... you already know what you are unable to do ... and that puts you firmly a step ahead of the pack ... and finally ... 8) you evaluate your progress ... the fire is out ... the ferries are gone ... you are a success ... what a Weasel ! ... you write in your mental self-evaluation ... the mill is piled in inflamous ashes with a heavy cloud upon its smoulders ... but hey ... if you try to please everybody you just make yourself miserable ... so join now ... if you can remember pages of lists ... and act independently without the support of outside logicsticks ... you just may be that special Weasel we are looking for ... think UNWFBEFAFRRSBST today !...

★ Motorized Mechanical Engine Duck ★

Oh ummm ... i've had've heard of these motorized mechanical engine ducks ... in books ... read about them at the movies ... browsed the television for historic cartoon tales of em too ... i could not believe my fuzzy weasel lights to be here ... like this ... alive and in weasel ... standing by the open door of one during actual events ... swallowing buckets

of prop wash ... half heard of hearing from the sound of its loud exsploittering ...

i checked that my plundles of parchments were not being blown amiss in many unwanton directions... but no ... they were safe in the short quick embrace of my very brief case ... i heard a familiar whirling which was just about off the tip of my recall ... but i could not replace it in my memory ... until another parch meant for me swirgled out the door and onto my nose ... this one was in weasel ... get in the plane you flipping weasel ... it read i read ...

★ Air Tidbit ★

Could it be me it was referring about ? ... i couldn't see any other weasel about ... i checked in true Weasel fashion with the old 720 degree spin around scan ... double checking we call it back in the Nests ... nope ... well, just in case, i hopped onto the board ... and slid into a seat with a stop ... it wasn't a crowded flight luckily ... so i got a seat nearby my hat ... the door bangled shut and bolted out the noise ... hey ... this was kind of pleasant ... i did what everybody does in the movies when they get themselves into one of these things ... i belted my buckle and looked for popcorn in the funny pouch on the back of the other seat up front there ...

there were only more papers and a funny bag ... and crumbs ... i nodded to my neighbrr ... no popcorn didja notice ? ... hey ... don't i know you from somewhere ? i cautioned ... i was answered with a whirl and another parch came floating ... i don't think so ... i read it read ... welcome to Air Tidbit ... A.T. is where its at ... sqweaked a funny box on the wall ... this is your pilot talking at you ... please distinguish out all bad karma and think good light airy happy floating thoughts now ... now ... now ... there was a lurch forward ... which caused a brief weighty darkish thought to brisk by ... but i swatted it and it fluttered better and more cheerful then ... the sqweak sqwackled again ... we will be flying approximately way up high because of all the mountains ... and very close to the speed of pretty quite fast ... and we are expected to be in the air until we arrive ... if you look out any of your windows you will have a greater chance of seeing one of Tidbit's very famous clouds than if you bury your nose in your pillow ... i decided to try another chat with the box across the aisle ...

★ Traveling Boxy Friend ★

Beg pardon ... i began ... i have this plundle of parchments ... what top hole what ? ... the deucable of it is ... i can't understand a scribble ... maps and decrees ... orders and commandments ... not got the figgiest ideal what who means ? ... this caused a bit of a whirl but no parchment came forth ... well ... at least we were making conversation ... its got me all in a bit of a fibble you see ... i added and stuffed the entire whole lot stocky barrel on top of my fellow traveling boxy friend ... here see what you can make of it ... i better go talk with the pilot ... good job on ya ... chin up ... sport ... i gave him the ol' weasel thumbs up ... some depreciate this simple gesture of appreciation ... but not the little folk ...

i didn't know contraptions could splutter ... or turn purple for that matter ... well ... i wouldn't worry over it ... it had plenty to keep itself busy while i was away ... i noticed my hat was smoking again ... this caused a darkening of my usually sunny sun glasses ... i thought i told you to stop ... but i had no time for a lecture right now ... i turned my attention to more important matters ... shouldn't they be serving snacks ? ... i rapped softly but decisively on the cotpit door ... which opened ... entirely against regulations and my nose for that matter ... ow ... i pried myself out and stuck my snout around the corner where i figured it belonged ... oops ... ow, again ... it got slapped ... but i knew that was going to happen ... i read it on the grapevine ... the one on the wine list on the door ... oh ... it was you know whom again ...

★ At The Cotpit ★

Say nothing about the weather for openers ... i repriminded myself ... hey its me ... remember me ? ... much better thanks and you ?... wow some amazing bumps you have turbulating in the Tidbit skies ... eh? ... whilmaswhiskers ! ... well at least this time i was forewarned ... i knew by now that spluggered was a word ... but the sqweak wasn't so smupffled ... i decided to jump right in before something else could expire ... where're we going ? ... couldn't help but

notice the beverage offerings ... will there be a sweets and cheese trolley after the main course ? ... perhopes a sniffer ? ...

ow ...well my sniffer wasn't doing so great ... the door shut against it again ... this time on its way closed ... must be a budget no thrills flight ... i headed back towards my chair carrying the wine menu just in case ... with a growing glowing nose ...

⋆ Nose Pumpkin ⋆

I found my well adjusted seat ... and reclined upon into it ... i reached for my plundles which i hoped by now were properly translittered ... oh ta ... said i ... oh and by the way while you're up ... here is the wine menu ... i gave him a nice self-service tip ... why do not you see if you can round up something in the tail ... rustle up some snacks and herd them up here ... good chap ... no no i will not hear of it ... off you go ...

geeznosepumpkins ... if you don't have anything nice to splutter don't splutter anything ! ... thanks very much ... why don't contraptions just keep it shut ? ... and to think i gave it its first real break ... keep up with the attirude and i'll be thinking of another big break i thought ... i rubbadubbed my nose ... ow that hurt ... indeed i had a small but tender pumpkin there ... nothing really halloweenish of course but undernerving neither-the-less ... i riffled a few raffles out of a tidy plundle and read on ...

Hmmm ... yes ... uh huh ... okay ... what ? ... purrpurrtraitors ? ... no ! ... catcomplices ? ... eh? ...i see ... yes ... uh huh ... miscellaneous indignation ... epidemic ... unethical ... okay .. dagoba ? ... Hindunothing Dacoits ? ... yes yes yes ... no ... no no ... diddle ? ...possibly ... daddle ! ... definitely ... oh umm ... this was getting nowhere ... i put the crossword down and picked up my raffles again ... sure okay ... they were painstakingly translitterated into weasel ... but whoever was the whom who thought weasels could follow or even read directions ... needed to first snort out their priorities in a fine row ...

i caught the drift tidily none-the-least ... it was not much different from the crossword puzzle now that you found me mentioning it ... odd that ... hmmm ... there was trouble in the upper highlands ... i had been paw picked due to my quality vocations ... somehow somewho had proactivated and kicked my deridossier back into action ... dang ... they found out about my especial secret serviette regimental training with the Weasel Highboggers ... the past had caught up with me at long last and was breathing tickly little hot puffs upon my neck ... my pal returned with a tray of goodies ... ah a nice Brrgundy ...now seemed a nice opportunity for a wee break ... i did have to go a bit ... and i already had my plundles all committed to memorabilia anyway ... due to my highly attuned and well poised weasel photogenic memory ... you see ... there came suddenly a jolt and lots of whirly sounds ... the plane pitched downwardly and my ears poppled ... the sqwackle announced ... we're ... we're ... oh my ... look out ! ... whew ... that was close ... uh ... we're going to ... what the devil ? ... argh ... what's wrong with this blasted thing ? ... to ... there was a loud thunk skip bunk and bump ... to ... land ... welcome to the Tidbit Higherhinteroutlands ...

⋆ Disembarkment ⋆

Thank you for flying with us ... Air Tidbit ... the only way to fly ... is in the air ... we hope to be seeing you up in it again soon ... please enjoy your stay here in nowhere ... hmmm ... well that didn't sound overly promising ... but at least the wine had tasted good ... like it always did before a tough assignment ... my nose pumpkin was receding and was no longer or even a squash ... just a tipped off orange glow ... things were looking good as we bumpled and scrimmaged to a halt ... it was a lovely day above the clouds ... but i noticed we had landed under them ... that weaselette pilot really does have an attitude i thought pensively ... i decided she had to lighten up a bit and needed stern words ... but i could not dole them out today ... today i was really busy now ... i would have to annoy her about it all later ...

i hopped out onto the disembarkment stairway and climbed to the top ... and waved a cheery wave in case anybody worth noticing was ... and took stockings of my dreary soreroundings ... i was in the early mournful rain without a dollup in my hand ... there was a cold brreeze ... luckily my clothing had returned to address me during the flight ... my bags had already been depositioned at the base of the steps ... hey wait a minute ... i left my stuff in my room at the Honey Bee ... could this be a sky pack jacking ? ... then i remembered the High Brr ...

⋆ Not Met On Assignment ⋆

Yes ... the Big Brr grrr... I growled ... this was not a pleasure cruise ... i was remindful of myself ... i was on assignment ... it was times like this that i wished i had joined the Piecemeal Core and had done some goodies in the world ... but no ... i bermed all those bridges in the daze of long ago ... it was all coming back to me now ... the training ... the endless hours of endodoctorization ... i could hear the relentless words of our old stiff sourgent ... what are you ! ... weasels weasels ! ... i can't hear you !... Weasels Weasels ! ... excuse me? ... WEASELS WEASELS ! ... yes you are ... NOT ! ... geezplatinumbskulls ... it was a wonder i ever lived through it ... any or all ...

i weaseled down the steps and onto the ice tarmac to retrieve my stuff ... i looked around to see if i would not be met ... the mechanical duck growled into life and splintered quickly way off to some other place to land from out of the sky at ... i watched it as it met the grey clouds trailed by puffs of its own ... there go my plundles ... i had only my memoirized files to riffle through now ... the rain was now snowing i noticed ... i felt foreloaned as if precious moments were fleecing me by by on borrowed time ... but then ... i always felt that way when not met on assignment ... now what i thought ... was unprintable by any standards ... but something printable was coming my way snaking in the wind ... perhaps my fortune to whistle a change ...

★ **Snow Matter What** ★

Okay one mr Weasel ... read the writing i read (that was pronounced red red on arrival .. not reed red .. or red reed .. nor neither reed reed .. as some may think) ... follow the arrow on this page ... it will lead you to the whereabouts you are being deployed out to ... what a lucky break ... up here all directions looked like relatives ... i could hardly tell them apart ... i could think i was headed great aunt Marge by third cousin Bob ... when in reality i was going directly towards due old uncle Harry ... i

didn't much fancy getting lost at this bleak stage of things ... the rain continued to pour down as snow ...

but snow matter what not ... that arrow seemed to point correctly right where i was going ... it was the dernedest thing ... it didn't even matter if i went in circles ... well if what they say about a room full of monkeys with typewriters and enough time is true

... i figured that i would eventually get to my destination in the next million years ... or at least be sending a letter to Weasilliam Shakestick's hamlet in the countryside ... hello Avon calling ... as usual the odds were in my flavour ... a million to one ... but of course i was that Weasel in a million ... except i still couldn't work out how the yellow polka dots had morffed from my undies to my outer pants ... like that ... most unsporting ... in my opinion ...

⋆ Dagoba Ruins ⋆

Well never mind ... i was all belled up to snuff and raring to know where i could go ... (although no suggestions were needed at this time from the gallery of peanuts) ... the arrow pointed to the up ahead ruins of an dagoba ... so i followed it ... this must be the one i had riffled about in my briefing on the Air Tidbit mechanical duck journey ... this could be where i would be meeting up with the Hindunothing Dacoits ... their methods were unethical i knew ... but we must not judge all everybodies by my high Weasel standards ... i entered flourishing throughout the in door with an announcement ...

hello my good foreign friendly pal buds ... i have met with my deployment obligations and am now fully introduced to here with duty in mind ... i did my duty on the plane earlier but i wasn't letting on ... do you have information on the purrpurrtraitors what have clawsed such an epidemic of miscellaneous indignations upon these lands ? ... come now ... i cannot diddle ... maybe dabble a bit ... but ... oops ... i was delving into my wrong mindful of listed memorizeds ... that was the crossword ... not my duty directions ... puzzling all this ... and disturbing in its silence ... i had an uneasy feeling about this place ...

PAWS 4

★ WEESSCOFF ★

Probably all of us share a close and intimate but uncuddly familiarity with the politiclamourous problems of our times ... but few of us are prepeppered to deal with their unpredictable cateredtastrophies ... a select group of wise weasels recognized the problem some years ago and established a tabletop secret training center to deal with this delicacy deficiency ... located at a location some mysterious where ...the Weasel Extra Especial Secret Serviette Commando Occupational Feisty Forces was created ... WEESSCOFF regularly inhales whimpy weasels and hacks them out into such solid products as the one pictured below ...

Wee Wambo Weasel came up thoroughly through and through the rank files ... earning honors alongst the ways and means ... WWW was reputed directly into WEESSCOFF and trained in subversive stanzas and other techniques of manners and poetic justice ... what side does the spoon go on ? ... our graduates know ... having trouble at important dinner parties ? ... our graduates can wipe up the mess ... do conversations turn sour over orange marmalade liver pâté luncheon tastings ? ... our graduates will lick things into shape ... is there waffling at your pancake feed ? ... our graduates will butter up the batter to give a clear margarine to your advantage ... all of your answers to these above questions should be a positive negatory No ! ... if you answered any in the Yes or Okay or i don't know or Roger That position ... you need to call the Weasel Extra Especial Secret Serviette Commando Occupational Feisty Forces* ... they'll have you for breakfast ... because that's what they graduated and are trained for ...

*satisfaction is not always quaranteened ... see the details ...

★ Yak Yak Yak ★

I couldn't quite place what made me feel so disquieted until i put my fingers on it ... ah ha ... yak yak yak ... that was it ... all this yak yak yakking and no sound ... no one was saying anything worth speaking about ... at least not yeti ... and i wasn't sticking about waiting for until they did ...

i assumed that i myself would be the hot topic of discussion ... and although i was in need of a little warmth ... i was thinking more of a nice toddy than to become grilled with verbals ... think transport i thought ... i had a long way to go ... assuming i was going anywhere ... so why not ride upon the backs of yawn yaks ... i would even have one to carry my tired old nap sack ... everyone would get a little shut eye and be refreshed in the morning ... for even as the clouds lifted and the snowing rain fizzled to merely a snizzle ... the sky above dimmed into evening ...

★ Twelve Hoof Power ★

So ... there i was ... all loaded up to the brim on a twelve hoof power yak pack chew chew train ... and headed into the deep unknownst of the brrly highlands at nearly six horns an hour ... by morning i calculated my outfit would be approximately seventy-two horns away from here ... me too ... for i swore my outfit with loyalty about myself ... except my hat which had its own headful of ideas and was a smidge untrustworthy ... but comfortable to be with none-the-lesson-learned ... it was nice to see my pants were giving me a break and had returned the yellow polka dots to my under garments ... i felt less conspicridiculous ... now ...

the night was fair to me ... raining a full sky of stars across a wide bright umbrella that dripped clear to the horizon not unlike the milky waves ... i even whistled a little tune ... Waltzing Wealdown Weaselettes ... this reminded me of the good long days of old ago ...i couldn't place any of them at the moment precisely ... but old ago was always great in the stories i told to get rid of annoying creatures ... well ... i thanked my lucky ear lobes there were none of those about now ... for i was annoyed enough wondering where all this yakking was leading us ... oh umm ... did weasels even have ear lobes ? ...

★ Fallen From Sleep ★

Well ... if they did .. then that was lucky ... but even if they didn't then that would be lucky too ... because then i wouldn't have to worry about not wearing earrings ... but this would all be different for the weaselettes whom really should by all rites have equal time in front of the mirror and lipstick vacuuming rights to vote powder puffy nose whiskers ... i awoke with a startled start ... great skittish Weasels ! ...

i must have dozed off ... no ... i looked at all and rounded myself ... no ... i was still on aboard yak which now did feel like a board ... i must have been a bored and fallen asleep ... well i couldn't have fallen far from my sad dell for whom tolls the wishing well come to my dreams it is so nice to see you hear me now for amour is in the air ... my head snapped up ... had i nodded off ? ... i looked all the way up and around ... no ... i was still on ... stage ... strutting the bored ... and they all loved me ... my wonderful lovely fans but now i must lease you dear things a new car ... and they were clapping and clapping and clipping and clap clopping clip clopping clip clopped to a stop ... i woke with a thump ... i must have a dozen of... one ... two ... six ... eight ... twelve ... hoofs ... this time i had fallen from sleep ...

★ Weasely Weasel Sniffs ★

Flip it ! ... right onto my nose as usual ... and i was just healing up my pumpkin too ... now i would probably have a whole vineyard of nose squash ... if i had to spend all of my time watering it ... i would be really irrigated and upset ... but all was alright for the ground was snowy soft where upon i fell and rose from the ashes ... i knealt and shook out a spinach almond pecatta noodle from my last pack of unfiltered Weasely Weasel Sniffs ... i lit one on a still

glowering ember and had a deep aeromatic therapuketic sniff ... it clears the sighnesses ... you see ... and this was real Weasely Weasel Sniff noodle country after all ... although some would say i wasn't really very much of a weasely Weasel sniffing spinach almond noodles rather than the nit picken gritty down to earth plain old spaghetti egg noodle sniffs like true weasely weasels do ... well everyone is entitled to their own opium ... i figgered ...

i felt the warm ashes ... others have been here before i surmised ... catnapping i bet ... less than a horn or so ago i calculated ... i placed my ear on the ground around and listened ... but all i could hear was mostly frozen dirt ... well no matter ... there were plenty of clue marks that had been well pawn over ... and some finely printed claws trailed from dust to dust and showed clearly the direction i must follow ...

★ A Fine Fair Mourning ★

For already a fine fair mourning was arising to smitten the heart of the night and bury it in coughins of rolling sunder clouds and rays ... at times like this ... i felt a lot of similarities with the great poet weasel explorers ... like Sir's Franchised Bacon ... but i was much too modest of myself to ever go public with me ... and in any case i must not be distracked from the rails of my purpose ... straight and true .. and level on the cue .. weasels wee weasels .. we know whom to get ... for anything to do ... an old hunting the plumbers song ... that keeps me of course if ever i tend to begin wandering from it ... i get all flushed when i sing it ... if only i could remember the tune ... there was a second verse ... some thing about pipe down Weasel ... but that escapes me as well nowadays ... was it similar to taps ? ... i wondered ...

well ... that was not of overt importance ... for there seemed to be a mutiny in progress ... the yaks would not yak a step further on ... they were apparently turning dagoba bound and making some rather rude noises by the way of departure ... my kip had been kaboodled in a heap ... but looked to be in pretty good kilter ... i was on my own ... me and my shadow ... hey wait a minute ... was i being followed ? ... i held down a brief wiggling panic that squirmed in the sinews of my vocal cords for a moment ... but when i turned to confront it ... my shadow stepped long into the open right in front of me ... oh ... i said ... you must be on my side ...

Well at least someone was ... it was early ... and there might be far to go ... or not ... i really didn't know for sure because i had never been here ... so i either better get going pronto ... or i had plenty of time and could take a nice long relaxing nap ... i was a bit of a professional compromiser ... so i took myself amongst the middle choice ... and ambled casually along ahead with my new shadey friend slithering silently along beside me ... not much fun this character ... i thought ... we followed the paws mutely for awhile while keeping out our wary eyes for the printers ...

i tried to ratchet up a simulating conversensation to help the time go by the clock ... i talked of mountains ... and shoes ... of rivers ... and socks ... of glaciers ... and the snore bored world championships ... of lakes ... and Weasely Weasel Noodle Sniffs ... of the great Lahassel bizarre ... and the legendary bargains available there ... i talked as i walked and he slithered ... and he slithered as i walked as i talked ... no matter of conversation was there that did not flow away from my eloquaint tongue ... and my words were of some obvious greatness ... for i seemed to swell in proportions in relation to my good quiet listening slithering pal ... by the time i had exhausted just a very minor smidgeon of my vast repertarry of topics ... the sun was high ... i looked for my good bud ... but good bud was not ... i checked under my feet but found nobudy ... just a couple of dark spots that were being cast down by my brim and brolly ... and to needle poke irritations more ... my hat was being a misbehaving cow polk and prodding those silly polka dots to morphalize again ...

⋆ Lonely Over The Top ⋆

I am very much afraid i have that awkward disappearing defect on people ... alas ... such is the fate of great numerous uno weasels like myself ... they say it is lonely over the top ... i decided there must be some grains of wisdom near what they say ... for i had been over the top for some time ... years maybe ... but i couldn't say if i was lonely as such ... not with such a vivid imagination clinging to me ... maybe a tad Companion Compatibility Challenged ... C

cubed syndrome i believe is the precise term used in medical cynics ... but please stop bothering me with irreverences and let me get back to my story ...

i carefully gauged the hour ... it must be nearly just about high noon for no buddy ... or a little after perhaps ?... for i already spied a wee shadey spot hanging about my left toe and looking a few minutes long ... i took stockade of my situation ... as usual i seemed to have arrived exactly where i was ...however ... the paws had trailed out ... and i was distemperairily shot with mystification ... dang ... where did they go ? ...

⋆ Total Sonar Eclipse ⋆

But i had precious small moments to wonder about it ... for i heard a great whooshing in the air as if a giant balloon was up there ... and then the sky darkened and all was quite quiescently quiet ... holy gummy gander bumps ... i had heard of these ... but i thought they were just myths ... lulls of reality ... anomalies of calm weather patterns ... like topical unhurricanes ... but now i was in the middle of one ... it

was a total sonar eclipse ! ... everything was mewt ...

wild rolling gravy tsunamis ... my multi-taskable flag array auto spannered itselves into a prop wash away modem ... many times i have been questioned why i carry my monastery colours so everywhere ... well for times like this ... of course ... its thoroughly modern modem mutts into a multitude of uses without having to wrench it manually ... instantly ... even in the dark ... if only i could blow these pushycats aside ... the landscape would slide into my wished for wash of sunbathing light ... a new day would flood dawn over the old one drenching it up to its nose in fond hopes ... and soundly too ... i hoped ...

★ If Only ★

If only i could purr severely ... i gripped my mod modem and gave it full throttle ... must hold on ... i thought ... can't let go ... so much depends on this ... must be strong ... sweat trickled onto my nose and started a dangerous tickle itch ... the inflection spread to my grip which twitched dangerously ... one finger was already making scritchy scratching motions ... others were all in favour with slight trembles ... would it come to a recall vote ? ... my nose inched forward ... maybe if i could just reach a paw nail ... but this put me dangerously off balance ... nose sweat dripped into my grasp like excess clutch fluid ... maybe just a wee centimeter more ... any takers on a millimeter or two ? ... my snout cried silently for relief ... the itch was high on nearly out of control ...

oops ... i passed over the invisible break even point ... my marginal ability of returns seemed to be slipping ... the prospurrous new dawning sunrise awakening was threatened ... it could end up just a sunruse instead ... but weren't we due for a upswing ? ... this could mean heavy bad quotes on importants and expected goods ... i could see an exodus of skilled wagerers leaving for foreign lands ... nothing short of a reactor of congress could stop these remarketable forces now ... it looked like futures all the way ... and my advice was to buy as if there were no tomorrow ... then sell low ... well its the way i became a great broker ... but if i was not steadfast now ... this could be another big break for me ... how uplifting of a prospect ... i thought ... then i discovered i hadn't a leg to stand on ...

★ Karmakazzie ★

But i knew my upforia would be short lived ... my clutch had been overtly sweated over ... it kept slipping on me with each shift of my gear ... tired right shoulder ?... shift pack and rest of gears to left shoulder ... i even tried reverse and neutral with no gear at all ... but there was no avail ... i was suddenly grasping thin air ... and fell with a thick sensation to below ... but bounced comfortably and threw snow to land in a tastefully decorated entresol with a nice cozy arm chair from which to watch the unfolding drama above ...

itwaspurekarmakazzie...myweaselmorffedstandardsversusthepurrpurrtraitor'spuffed balloon ... there would be no winner here ... but this could well be the season's big sun block buster ... i slipped my 3D coloured lens over my specs ... and sipped a soda ... with any luck this would be a very illuminating experience ...

PAWS 5

★ Down And Out ★

Hello ... welcome to Burned 'em Notably Book Night Guesthouse ... where you can read while you sleep while we pick your pockets for you ... as if in the comforts of your own home ... we are very puddled to have with us this tonight at long lasso ... the very flamuous and controversed poet lariat Count Weasel Von Der Veasel ... from deep within the dark and mysterious Snorteast Europing Hinderlands .... and without farther adieus ... i present you your standard Von Der Veasel author ... for a one night only candle light reading ... clap clap clap ... clap clap ...

no ... no ... please keep the clap trap for your prisoners of established thought ... save it for the those who art caught in the confinements of social unjuicyness ... i am much much too humble ... your awed and worshipping hushed gawks coupled vif envious ears ... is more becoming for one such as i ... thank you ... i vill now read from my award vinning appendrix of upper di-dactyl pentathoholic rhymes ... as immortalized in my titled collection ... which is reasonably priced to customairily match each individuals intellectual gullibility temperament ... and purse ...

<u>Its a Weasel's Life : or Down and Out in London and Paris and Lisbon and Athens and Cairo and New York and Delhi and Kabul and Shaktoolik and Abu Dubai and Zanzibar and Hong Kong and Sydney and Rome and Valletta and Rabat and Marseilles and Stockholm and Karachi and Prague and Vienna and Copenhagen and San Jose and Oslo and Knossos and Antioch and Tallahassee and Tenerife and Jerusalem and Salem and Tripoli and Kaikora and Nome and Johannesburg and Antikythera and Baghdad and Wasilla and Seoul and Toronto and Kaltag and Istanbul and Beirut and Los Angeles and Amman and Queenstown and Doha and Beijing and Khartoum and Moscow and Damascus and Fujieria and Yellow Knife and Lima and Hanalei and Wellington and Alice Springs and Ruby and Bombay and Vancouver and Dublin and Jebel Ali and Godalming and Hamilton and Penryndydreth and Dunkirk and Luxembourg and Belem and Austin and Philadelphia and Benghazi and Nelson and Iskanderun and Nenanna and Piraeus and Monaco and Innsbruck and Gaza and Equitos and Homer and Glastonbury and Boulder and Minto and Palmyra and Saint Petersburg and San Moritz and Seward and Weaslton and Cadbury and John O'Grotes and Berlin and Petra and Green River and Ras Shukair and Tyler and Jezziene and Goteborg and Houma and Medina and Moose Pass and Alexandria and Skopje and Sharjah and Sidon and Cripple Creek and Thessalonica and Well Just About Every Which Where But Up.</u>

and i quote ... ahem ... "hey ? what gives?" ... thank you very much for coming tonight ... clap clap ... clap clap clap ... no no ... didn't i say to keep your clap shut ... you fools ... ah ... my poor fans ... they do adore me so ... copies of this great work can be obtained into the sweety clutches of your very own paws by sending unwanted cash ... checks ... or money orders to :

        The Weasel
        c/o the Von Der Veasel
        Rue Nom de Plume 13 A étage 3
        New Weaslton   SW 007
        Unified Kinsdom of Great Nestian

★ Balloon Popple ★

And it was ... in less than this instance the heavens were rent ... and at a good price too ... shards of balloon were poppled in all directions ... and misconstrewn from on high to swing low sweetly ... my monastery standards went flags over pole into the great vow of silence with an excellent self sacrificial praying mantra ... i shed a tear ... and was nearly moved to applause ... if only my old monk key group could see this ... need more be said ? ... they probably all had a third eye glimpse anyway ... and were already scouring the country side waving each and every banner looking for the true reincarnations of these four wise flags ... i of course wished them luck ...

the day brightened with an instant flash as if the sun had just opened up its rays for all to unfold and be beholden for ... a bit irradiating ... i thought but i always purrfurred the slow cat's meow of a gradual sunrise tinting along at a colorful pace ... rather than this outlandish exploitation of blinding glitter ... well ... its all a part of the show ... i reminded myself ... and took it with good cheer ... the 3D effects were great ... and what a story ! ... it made me feel warm all over ... especially the part about the far flung kittypoos ...

★ Big Champion Ships ★

But now what ? ... i thought ... a great show and all ... with the exploition of sun rays ... and disincarnated flags ... and flying kittypoos ... but where standst i in all this ? ... i stood up ... but i felt like my own bubble had been poppled instead of some silly balloon ... wasn't there something about a snore bored mission missing here? ... i heard a distant growl on the far air sky ... had the kittys figured out that they should be annoyed by the recent turn of events ? ... they were rather slow after all ... but no ... it was something else ... something red ... i read ...

big champion ships ... this way ... well ... this was a turn of events ... it has been years since my knavey days ... but i was always a sucker for the big boats ... tall sails ... wind a bit cheeky ... salt in my whiskers ... you probably wouldn't know it now ... but i was once quite the weasel of the seven high oceans ... tally ho what ? ... and all that horn jig pipe rot ... but why by captain's cook's cupboards were they up here on the steppes ? ... i would have thought down by the seaside would be more appropriated ... maybe they knew something i was not in the know about ... i decided to follow ...

★ Hey Wait Up Down ★

But i was on paw ... and the sign in sky was trotting along at many horse powered miles per gallop ... it was already at least a hopalong cloud cluster ahead ... there wasn't any part of me included in the way of catching up at this unfair rate ... plus the basket case of puttykits had been flung on even further in the same similar direction already too ... i called ... hey wait up ! ... down ...

for indeed i was hollering below ... the sky high scribbles and motorized red flying puller plane was just ducking far out out of sight man ... my eyes were not deceiving themselves oddly enough ... for they were seeing normal visions of a hidden valley lying directly to my face as if untrue ... could this really be where the armada was ? ... i looked closer but no inland sea could be sawn from where i was stumped ... then things got more familiar ...

★ The Shangri La La Lawless Nests ★

Well ... if this didn't just fry the cake wok ... usually i don't put up with familiarity ... but i had seen a videidiotic documockery about this place once upon some livingroom ago ... but from the way it was presented on the telejellovision ... i thought it was really just a reality show about some disco dive in Lost Weasangleaf or something ... but here it was impersonation ... lying through the teeth of the feet of a great big massive massif glacier ... the mysticalibrated valley of the Shangri La La Lawless Nests ... seen in this sinking light really didn't do it justice ... i thought ... but then that probably had something to do with the low down battery of La La lawyers that were supposed to keep the place running and online ... for shirley there was something too not write about here ... nor for anyone else for that matter ...

this was a scary place where only the laurelled and hardy could eek out a living ... no wonder the basketed terracattas were coming to earth here ... i would have to watch my step along the path now ... for the locals practiced rarely exotic and perplexifying forms of Confusionism ... and if crossed by ignorants or on purpose ... their temper trampolines could turn extremely bouncy ... and that was the elastic thing i wanted to start at this jingle of time ...

★ Double Oh Double You ★

But if i kept a mindful there would be little chance of that ... i reminded myself of my ignormous duty to my snore bored mission as decreed by monsignor the High Brr himself ... whatever it was ... it was primadonna on my mind ... i would have to ooze through the crowds like a secreted agent ... double oh double u ... oh oh you you Weasel ! ... as Vana used to say ... or OOW ! ... as i used to say when i snubbed my toe accidentally on something hardy ... i darkened my garb to suit the suituation thing ...

firstly i would pick up the trail and follow my nose ... to wherever it was scent ... my next port of call ... after a quick nip into the loo ... would be the Ice Cat Plaids ... where people congratulate in large groups is where i would find answers ... questions ... mysteries ... and perhaps a pizza the brewing action ... i really should have had some kind of musicy theme background tune to go with this part ... but i was on my own ... with no symphony for my dramatic soloing lonely travail ... how little the world cares about the shadowy weasel spy world ... i lamented ... but i shrugged it off ...

⭐ Well Cornered ⭐

Because that is the way it is ... in the weasel candlelit clandestined world of cloak cloek cloik clook clouk and sometimes cloyk and dagger degger digger dogger dugger and sometimes dygger ... blast it all ... it seems so unfayr sometimes ... but that is

what we are paid forgetting info ... anyway the weaselettes think it is very cool even if i do draw a lot of heat ... well here i was well cornered for viewing on some lonely stretch of the route ... an uneasy turn and a twist away from the brunt of the crowd ... whom curb together en mass under brighter lights ... i read my complimentary program card by the light of a La La City sidewalk candle ...

the Ice Cat Plaids parade should be passing by at any momentum ... i felt a little like i was backstaged here ... but there would be advantages for being so positioned ... the weaselettes usually wait to adjust delicate matters of the costume varieties when not in the bright light glare of the lime ... but would it be too dangerous to try and reach my contacts now ? ... i decided in the affirmative ... my glasses would have to do ...

★ The Miss Media Float ★

The Miss Media float was beginning to full swing around the corner preceded by confetti and some paper stringers ... would Vana be here ? ... i hopped beyond hope for a glimpse ... but ended up trompling my own tail ... and gave it up ... let's see i saw something in the program about this ... yes yes ...

here it was ... a list of near Misses ...

Miss Quoted ... Miss Understood ... Miss Spelt ... they were all here ... Miss Judged ... Miss Printed ... Miss Read ... Miss Placed ... wow ... this was big stuff ... i felt a little out of place myself ... a rough around the edges weasel public private ear like myself in such distinguished company ... but i was in cogs .. neat .. oh .. and well groomed too ... i was pretty indiscrete ... i would draw little attention ...

★ In The Clear But Not ★

Or so i thought ... i was busy tabulating a series of unconfirmed reports of unconnected eyewitness encounters ... for future referencing ... when i noticed that i of all weasels had become a focal point of attention ... this was not right ... i wasn't Miss anything ... or had i missed something ? ...

my first reaction was to get out of focus ... so i tried to blurr my image a bit ... i set the ambiance controls to time exposure and opened the f stop wide ... that should do the trick ... while i just nip off into a vanishing point somewhere down the alley ... or so i thought ... but some whom had preconsidered my every moves and had readjusted the asa-iso numbers for the reality film ... i was still in the clear ... when i should have be in the clear by now ... but wasn't ... since i was ...

★ Shangri La Highed ★

What the ? ... i abruptly wondered ... but i then saw what was going on and why the interests were on me ... the Snore Bored Champion Ships were loading ... and i was being waited on ... as i always figured i should be ... hand and foot ... but hey ? ... not like this ... what're y'all doing ? ... unhand me you villains ! ... you foul La La lawless ruffians ! ... this is against the lawn of the land ! ... i had green stains on my rear drive to prove it ... a not very couth foot booted me on bored ... but i struggled valiantly ...

i could scarcely believe my thoughts that were clamouring against all cognition of what my doubting eyes were seeing so apparently ... i was being Himal mountain Shangri La Highed in Tidbit somewhere ... but this was all wrong ... my expertise was needed on the slopes ... i couldn't let the team down now ... after all i had been through ... i could snore bored from awake to breaking the soundly asleep barrier in less than 0 to 60 seconds ... i was famous for it ...

I better tell them ... i'm very famous ... i told them ... but they weasel handled me down the hatch and into the breadbox ... to be held in a crumby hold ... a few of my close confettirates followed me down ... well they have heard of me in Weaslton ! ... i shouted ... but my shouts fell unsliced on hard baked sourdough ears ... i tried another tactic ... i'm the Weasel from WICO ! ... you know ... the Weasel Intelligence Company Operations ... i know tricks ! ...

but only sound came as laughing voices that filtered through another doorway ... the sound of cash being boxed in the other room purrcolated ominously ... hushed murrpurrs were poured by the cupful ... they ranneth over ... and then were stirred around ... presumably with a spoon of honey and a tad of milk ... it sounded like i was missing something ... chocolate crumb cheesecake? ...

PAWS 6

★ The Weasels Of Basketville ★

Hello my very very good friends ... during the following paws you may be understood to be subjected to some intense and troubling information ... much of which could be viewed as if by disturbed individuals ... i hereby relinquish any and all of my rights that i may never or ever have had or have have pertaining to them ... so we here at Bubbled Weasel Productions would like to reconfirm that you the reader are reading this sentence ... because if since you are ... that lawfully means that you read the previous red sentence ... which is legally binding in case you decide later to come courting the law ... by reading the disclaimer red sentence ... we have unanimally agreed that you are not permitted to sue ... thereby leaving said Weasel outfit unholdable nor accounted able for any or all conceivable conditions resulting from the readers readings ... thanks so much ...

it is a tiny unknown fact that the howling mad Weasels of Basketville were probably not very committed ... which means of course that with such lackluckster standards they may have gotten loose ... or even possibly are loose ... the implications for the unwary public are so suspectacular that even sure locked homes are not completely safe ... the weasely critters could be up .. over .. or underwear anywhere at any time ... ready to pop out and cause a frightening scarcity even when you least expected of it ... panic is probably your best bet ... but many people just become jitter buggy eyed nervfussy and check behind their backs incessantly ... others even start pear annoyed fruity behaviors thinking a nut case could foam right out of the mouth of their refrigerator at them ... others get to cranking out bad moodulating swings or even more serious epidermantics ... but like we said ... alas ... you read the disclaimer ... we are holding blameless here ... we just wanted to let you know the game is a foot ... and that any time ... those scritching noises ... that any who ... those mupfled sqweaks ... that any how ... there could be a Basketville Weasel coming to git yew ...

custom neurotic responses can be obtained and hand tailored for the reader's special needs by sending said reader's money to:

Doctor Wat Song Weasel
c/o the Ole Peasoop Fog
Wondon Road near Feet Street
Wondon, Weasangleland WC 10

★ The French Fried Foreign Legion ★

I crept to the door to invite myself ... when ... mon dieu ! ... i made out the accents ... these creatures were from the French Fried Foreign Legion ... i was out of the oil pan and into the frit fryer for sure now ... a few hot ones landed nearby ... but i wasn't having any of it for the moment was too at hand ... a faintly familiar sqweak waffled in ... it sounded a bit like that weaselette driver pilot ... the one with the mal attitude outlook on life ... but why would she be here exchanging money ? ... why wasn't she at the bank ? ... there was an answering vocalization ... oui oui oui ... we ... we will carry out your instructions ... good bye bye ...

her instructions ? ... what was this ? ... could such a fair gal be in cat-hoots with such scumdrels as this ? ... she must have been brain washed and hung out to dry to sink so low ... she needs a good wringing ... i thought ... i will definitely have to iron this out before it all comes out in the wash later ... but right now i had pressing matters on my hands ...

★ The Obviator ★

I must escape or spend the next part of forever in the far sands of the Sohairy Desert ... a fashionating place for model tourists ... but not for pommefritting about en march with the French Frys under hot fire from hostile native Sohairian tribes ... i didn't want my own memorial pentagram twinkling dully in the constellation of fallen stars embedded in the sidewalks of le Champs de Lizards in Parie ... or was that Wollyhood where they did that ? ... not in this life time anyway ... mais pas non ! ...

i decided to obviate my way out of this fixture ... i obtruded into the open with a decisive obbligato ... obverted my nose to avoid detection and obstructions ... and obvoluted up the stairs ... such an obvious move was lost on my obtuse catptors who were obliviously lost in an obtected huddle mewing obsessed obloquies over their ill rotten gotten gain again and again ... nothing denser than a french fried catfritter ... i thought ...

★ Oar Snore Paddle ★

I shuffled like a card to the top of the deck ... and felt a good breast of fresh air like with a slap on the cheek ... i ran to the railing ... the Champion Ships were both already underway ... with me and without me ... i would have to get off this one in order to get to the right one ... before i would be for gone and left behind at the same time ... i decided to purple up my jump suit a cheerful smidge ... and jump ship ... or ... or ... ? ...

oar ... well i was quite an oarator after all ... so to speak ... so i grabbed the nearest one and hopped overboard into awake awash with snow ... what an entrance this will be ... i thought ... jumping right into a difficult technical one footed triple jokulhlaup cowchow with a classic death spiral twist ... i could see the headlines ... Oratorical Weasel Oar What ? ... i would probably even get an extra award for the innovigorating new design ... the patent-pretending Oar Snore Paddle ...

★ Finnished Record ★

But future glory ... though only a shoe in the matter of moments way ... would have to take a back seat on the handle while i concentrated on my every move ... the common weasel in the aisle would not notice little technical error mistakes ... but the judges surely would ... as i rocketed it through the final gates of the course with alluring precision ... i thought ... what a cinch ... a quick vision of myself opening an endorsement for Coca-Coocoo-Weasel-Up soda pop whiskled half fast past my mind in a blurrb ... the High Brr Nation toast of the town ... showers of fermented bubbly ... i was really rocking out this time ... and suddenly i was ... after i hit a big one right nearby the finnish line ...

well ... i knew this was going to be one of my better runs ... it just felt right spiritually ... i had been peeking at my aggressive potential performenace lately ... and could see i was primed for expressing speed ... my carbs were cooking abs and burning thighs right up to the mesmersizable nutritional edge ... i was pushing the limit of my sweat-wicking abrasion-irresistant workhorse-breathable all-ready weathered garment gear ... to say nothing about my world clash oar ... i maintained shrewd clear goals by aiming just that epic bit higher threw out and up ... little did i know that i would be settling the new finnished record ...

★ New High Score ★

But there it was ... up on the score bored to tiers ... eighteen feet and twenty-nine inches in a minute and sixty-two point zero zero zero zillionths of a second ... wow ... not just a finished record ... but a broken one too ... smashed ...

at times like this i always feel elated and up in the air ... but today i also actually

felt a tad broken up about everything ... my mission was accomplished ... the competition had been petted completely over ... the unethical epidemic of miscellaneous indignation of the dreadful catcomplices seemed to have scurvied off the upper highlands on a pirated champion ship ... the High Brr would be pleased ... for i was well done ... so why did i get the feeling i was in for a big let down after all this ?

⭐ Tail Spun ⭐

I must be a partial psychic delicate thinking weasel ... for no sooner had i thought this thought than my premonition monitioned into motion ... down i came in a tail spin to a crestfallen heap ... i must have caused a bit of a depression when i landed ... for my spirits came tumbling after ... am i blue ? ... well some parts were ... others were black and blue ... some great reward this is ... i thought ... i got the daylights savings knocked right out of me ...

i checked my watch ... spring forward ... fall back ... well i had sprung forward an hour ... ago ... or so it seemed ... and i be leaf it was starting to spring all around me too ... there was a daisy ... a daffoiled lily ... a good ole bud ... but the fall back shouldn't have happened till autumn ... oh well ... i was always a bit out of time and steppes when you came down on top of it all ... nothing really hurt ... i wagged my extremity to be sure ... and ... oh my gosh ago ... my winter's tail was coming to an end ... it was already returning half past brown ...

⭐ Dis Appearance Disappears ⭐

And soon my camofudging would be visible to all ... for snow still lay rampant upon the ramparts of the steppes ... and storms could be expected to rampage in white shades even up to the very edge of browned summertime... and i ... a humble moderately darkish beige weasel of the low down rolling plain fields below ... was autometiculously fixated to an early coat exchange rate ... my futures were bid ... bought ... and soon to be delivered ... i could end up the only weasel yakking around about bull in a Brr bear marketplace ... a brownie on a pale icing background ...

a dangerous situation to find one self same Weasel in in the upper Tidbitten highlands
... at this rate of exchange an impending trample seemed absolsosurely certain ... for
to be found out in the open with such a prominent profile ... one nose it is snaught but a
calling card to become a tasty mooshed tidbit myself for some unscrupulousy catizen ...
and so ... very much against my will ... i was afraid i must be forced fled from here on out
of here ... i could appear no longer on this stage of the round about ... dis winters tail ...
dis appearance ... must had to become a whole new disappearance ... once again ... and so
... alas of alacks ... i caught the very next running board silly and away ...

but that is a nutter story ...

Paws 7

☆ Doctored Sigweasel Froid ☆

There are many many ways to deal with rising panic ... as it wells up from the misty
serious places deep down inside the psychic somewhere ... as it wiggles its way through
the complexes trying to pop out anywhere it can ... nose ... eyes ... attitude ... mouth ...
all are tell tail risk points ... we must first recognize the problem ... then get handlebars
on it ... and come to grips with it before it comes to gripes ... yes my friends its our
old problem popping up again ... i think your nose of what i speak ... for i have seen to it
too ... Weasel Addictified Withdrawal Accumulation Mentally Activated Mind Addled
Syndrome ...
yes ... WAWAMAMAS ...

don't try to deny it ... it only makes it harder to weasel out of things ... and that's what its all about ... isn't it really ? ... but lucky for all you sufferers ... there is stirring new hope being mixed up in with the rest of the garbled flotsam that jetsams the current twisted canals and tributarries of your minds ... and i am here to help turn the spoon ... me ... your selfless same renowned care giver ... Doctored Sigweasel Froid ... official cool psychoticanalyst of the High Brr himself ... awarded the Very Cross Medals of Honorable Intentions and Penthoused Up Dreamy Frustrations ... a heart to heart donor of unsurpassed psychoillogical transplanted advice ... a well respected sleeping Libido dancer and Idioptical choreographer from long ego ... what lies are lying about in your subunconscious nest playing havoc with misconceptual symbols and spreading problems onto the surface of your daily life ? ... fear not afflicted folks ... i can let them loose for you ... between commercials of course ... using my new Modulating Modern Mind Model Molding Methods ... i call it my Sextet-M-Up plan of action ... all you do is lie down and babble off to sleep ... and while you sleep ... i pry to make sense of your dreams ... It's that easy ... no drugs or electrical shocks ... no dips in freezing water ... no operations ... sounds to good to be true ? ... there has to be a catch ? ... believe it or not there hasn't been one yet ... i'm still free ... except of course for your fee ...

appointments are accepted only with prepayments ... please call : 1-8000-555-FROID or FAX your bank account number and and/or or your credit card number with your signature and birthday date to : the Weasel @ 1-8000-555-FRAUD ... you will receive a prompt thank you card with probable new zero-balance account privileges all included ...

Episode Awards 3
★ **Weasel Meal Ticket Too Wide** ★

Let it not be known that the readers of Book Three of the Weasel Chronicles : A Winter's Tail have not appreciated in values to us ... nor that Bubbled Weasel Productions doesn't not depreciate your true devalued worthlessness ... not mostly in the least at all ... for this is neither the case nor not neither either was it never ... so in order to show you now how our true feelings really are not about the matter having not developed ... we have significantly and deliberately thoughtlessly overexposed your feelings to all and sundry and monday ... then we dedicated them to the far back burner and returned up the heat with this special presentation of a free uncomplimentary Weasel Meal Ticket Too Wide ...

this could very well be a very well upward taken ring of the rungs of the ladder of life for our standard reader ... and family too ... for the free Weasel Meal Ticket Too Wide is good for everybody fat saturated or not that the holder wants to be holding it for * ... good and bad cholesterol privileges at major participating airport lounges are part parcel and packaged in the deal as well ** ... full virtual citizenship-like menu choice voting rights go along with the included signature club time share in all particpatient countries *** ... ticket validity may expire with the user or before ****...

*   polly unsaturated crackers may be not included depending on market fat   factors ...
**   unless they are not parceling out at some major hubs ...
***   usually ...
****   if user widens to a midrift - height ratio width of two to one the wide is usually considered nul and over ...

Printed in the United States
by Baker & Taylor Publisher Services